KIDS ON EARTH

Wildlife Adventures – Explore The World
Sifaka Lemur - Madagascar

Sensei Paul David

COPYRIGHT PAGE

Kids On Earth: Wildlife Adventures - Explore The World

Sifaka Lemur - Madagascar

by Sensei Paul David,

Copyright © 2023.

All rights reserved.

978-1-77848-177-2 KoE_WildLife_Amazon_PaperbackBook_madagascar_sifaka lemur

978-1-77848-176-5 KoE_WildLife_Amazon_eBook_madagascar_sifaka lemur

978-1-77848-419-3 KoE_Wildlife_Ingram_Paperbackbook_SifikaLemur

This book is not authorized for free distribution copying.

www.senseipublishing.com

@senseipublishing
#senseipublishing

Synopsis

This book provides 30 unique and fun facts about Sifaka Lemurs, a species of primate found in Madagascar. It covers topics such as their diet and habitat, behavior and social structure, adaptations, lifespan, and more. The book also explains why Sifaka Lemurs are endangered, and provides an introduction and conclusion to the book. By the end of the book, readers will have a better understanding of this incredible species and a newfound appreciation for Sifaka Lemurs.

Get Our FREE Books Now!

 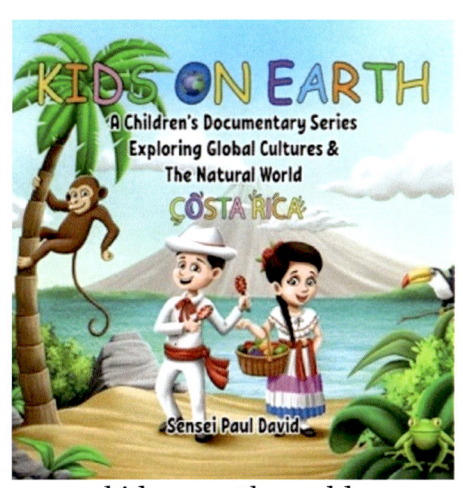

kidsonearth.life   kidsonearth.world

Click Below for Another Book In Each Series

senseipublishing.com/KoE_SERIES

senseipublishing.com/KoE_Wildlife_SERIES

KoE En Español

senseipublishing.com/KoE_SERIES_SPANISH

www.senseipublishing.com

Join Our Publishing Journey!

If you would like to receive FUTURE FREE BOOKS and get to know us better, please click www.senseipublishing.com and join our newsletter by entering your email address in the pop-up box.

Follow Our Blog: senseipauldavid.ca

Follow/Like/Subscribe: Facebook, Instagram, YouTube: @senseipublishing

Scan the QR Code with your phone or tablet to follow us on social media:

Like / Subscribe / Follow

Introduction

Welcome to the world of Sifaka Lemurs! Sifaka Lemurs are an incredible species found in the wild in Madagascar. These fascinating animals are truly unique, and there is much to learn about them. In this book, you will discover 30 fun and interesting facts about Sifaka Lemurs and learn why they are so special. From their diet and habitat to their behavior and social structure, this book will give you a better understanding of this incredible species. So let's dive in and explore the wonderful world of Sifaka Lemurs!

Sifaka Lemurs are primates, which means that they are related to humans and other primates like chimpanzees and gorillas.

Sifaka Lemurs live in the tropical rainforest of Madagascar, where they spend their days swinging from the trees and eating leaves, fruit, and other plants.

Sifaka Lemurs are very social animals and live in groups of up to 30 individuals.

Sifaka Lemurs are very good at leaping and can jump up to 20 feet in one jump!

Sifaka Lemurs have special adaptations for surviving in the rainforest, such as strong claws for climbing and a prehensile tail for gripping branches.

Sifaka Lemurs have a unique way of communicating with each other using vocalizations, body language, and facial expressions.

Sifaka Lemurs are primarily herbivores, meaning they feed mainly on plants.

Sifaka Lemurs have a lifespan of up to 25 years in the wild.

Sifaka Lemurs are diurnal, which means they are active during the day and sleep at night.

Sifaka Lemurs can be very territorial and will protect their territory from other lemurs.

Sifaka Lemurs have special adaptations for living in the trees, such as long, powerful legs and long tails for balancing.

Sifaka Lemurs have an interesting form of locomotion called vertical clinging and leaping, which allows them to move quickly through the trees.

Sifaka Lemurs have a diverse diet and will eat a variety of fruits, leaves, flowers, and even insects.

Sifaka Lemurs will occasionally eat small animals, such as lizards and frogs.

Sifaka Lemurs have an interesting mating system in which males compete for females and form harems of up to five females.

Sifaka Lemurs have a gestation period of about five months and usually give birth to one or two young.

Sifaka Lemurs are very vocal and can make a variety of vocalizations, including grunts, barks, squeaks, and whistles.

Sifaka Lemurs have a special grooming behavior called "allogrooming", which is when two lemurs groom each other.

Sifaka Lemurs are highly intelligent and can learn to recognize individual faces and recognize certain symbols.

Sifaka Lemurs are endangered due to habitat loss and hunting, and there are less than 10,000 left in the wild.

Sifaka Lemurs have a unique form of locomotion called "doubling", where they leap from tree to tree with both arms and legs.

Sifaka Lemurs have a unique form of social play called "stink fighting", where they wrestle and squirt each other with a foul-smelling liquid.

Sifaka Lemurs have a unique form of courtship behavior called "singing duets", where two lemurs will sing back and forth to each other.

Sifaka Lemurs are very tactile and will often groom each other as a form of social bonding.

Sifaka Lemurs have a unique form of "playful aggression", where they will wrestle and chase each other in a playful manner.

Sifaka Lemurs have an interesting form of communication called "stink marking", where they rub their scent glands on branches and leaves to mark their territory.

Sifaka Lemurs are very social animals and will often form strong bonds with each other.

Sifaka Lemurs have a unique form of communication called "smacking", where they

Sifaka Lemurs are very acrobatic and will often do flips and somersaults while leaping from tree to tree.

Sifaka Lemurs are an amazing species and are truly one of a kind!

Conclusion

We hope you enjoyed learning about the wonderful world of Sifaka Lemurs! From their diet and habitat to their behavior and social structure, these fascinating animals are truly unique and full of fun facts. We hope that you now have a better understanding of this incredible species and perhaps even a newfound appreciation for Sifaka Lemurs.

Thank you for reading this book!

If you found this book helpful, I would be grateful if you would **post an honest review on Amazon** so this book can reach other supportive readers like you!

All you need to do is digitally flip to the back and leave your review. Or visit amazon.com/author/senseipauldavid click the correct book cover and click on the blue link next to the yellow stars that say, "customer reviews."

As always…

It's a great day to be alive!

Share Our FREE eBooks Now!

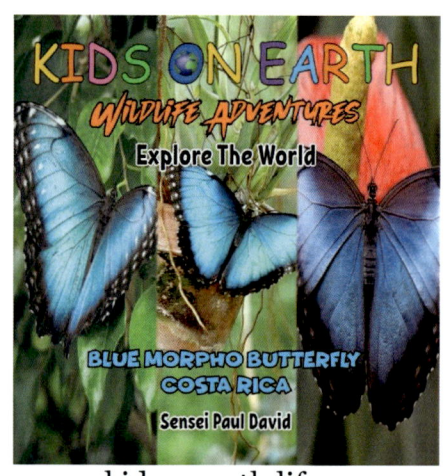

kidsonearth.life

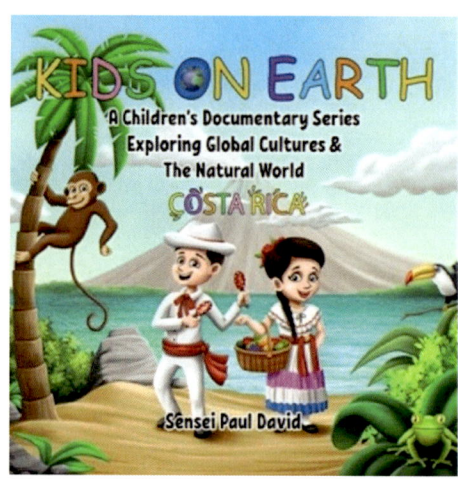

kidsonearth.world

Click Below for Another Book In Each Series

senseipublishing.com/KoE_SERIES   senseipublishing.com/KoE_Wildlife_SERIES

KoE En Español

senseipublishing.com/KoE_SERIES_SPANISH

www.senseipublishing.com

www.senseipublishing.com

@senseipublishing
#senseipublishing

Check out our **recommendations** for other books for adults & kids plus other great resources by visiting
www.senseipublishing.com/resources/

Join Our Publishing Journey!

If you would like to receive FREE BOOKS and special offers, please visit www.senseipublishing.com and join our newsletter by entering your email address in the pop-up box

Follow Our Engaging Blog NOW!
senseipauldavid.ca

Get Our FREE Books Today!

Click & Share the Links Below

FREE Kids Books

lifeofbailey.senseipublishing.com
kidsonearth.senseipublishing.com

FREE Self-Development Book

senseiselfdevelopment.senseipublishing.com

FREE BONUS!!!
Experience Over 25 FREE Engaging Guided Meditations!

Prized Skills & Practices for Adults & Kids. Help Restore Deep Sleep, Lower Stress, Improve Posture, Navigate Uncertainty & More.

Download the Free Insight Timer App and click the link below:
http://insig.ht/sensei_paul

About Sensei Publishing

Sensei Publishing commits itself to helping people of all ages transform into better versions of themselves by providing high-quality and research-based self-development books with an emphasis on mental health and guided meditations. Sensei Publishing offers well-written e-books, audiobooks, paperbacks, and online courses that simplify complicated but practical topics in line with its mission to inspire people toward positive transformation.

It's a great day to be alive!

About the Author

I create simple & transformative eBooks & Guided Meditations for Adults & Children proven to help navigate uncertainty, solve niche problems & bring families closer together.

I'm a former finance project manager, private pilot, jiu-jitsu instructor, musician & former University of Toronto Fitness Trainer. I prefer a science-based approach to focus on these & other areas in my life to stay humble & hungry to evolve. I hope you enjoy my work and I'd love to hear your feedback.

- It's a great day to be alive!
Sensei Paul David

Scan & Follow/Like/Subscribe: Facebook, Instagram, YouTube: @senseipublishing

Scan using your phone/iPad camera for Social Media
Visit us at www.senseipublishing.com and sign up for our newsletter to learn more about our exciting books and to experience our FREE Guided Meditations for Kids & Adults.

www.ingramcontent.com/pod-product-compliance
Lightning Source LLC
Chambersburg PA
CBRC090902080526
44587CB00008B/171